FOR OFFICIAL USE ONLY.

$\frac{121}{8905}$

Supplement (Provisional) to Instructions issued 8th January, 1916,

ON

THE OFFENSIVE OF SMALL UNITS.

BY

GENERAL HEADQUARTERS, EASTERN ARMIES,
27th September, 1916.

Summarized from the French and issued by the General Staff, December, 1916.

The Naval & Military Press Ltd

Published by

The Naval & Military Press Ltd
Unit 5 Riverside, Brambleside
Bellbrook Industrial Estate
Uckfield, East Sussex
TN22 1QQ England

Tel: +44 (0)1825 749494

www.naval-military-press.com
www.nmarchive.com

In reprinting in facsimile from the original, any imperfections are inevitably reproduced and the quality may fall short of modern type and cartographic standards.

SYNOPSIS.

PARAS.		PAGE
1–6	NEW ORGANIZATION OF COMPANY TO BE ADOPTED TO SUIT NEW WEAPONS AND NEW METHODS ...	4
4	1st half-section—	
	No. 1 squad—grenadiers (hand-grenade men and grenade gunners) ...	4
	No. 2 squad—fusiliers (automatic riflemen) ...	4
	2nd half section—	
	No. 3 squad—voltigeurs (or rifle men)	5
	No. 4 squad—ditto	5
7–17	CHARACTERISTICS OF NEW WEAPONS—	
8	Hand-grenade—in defensive	5
9	in offensive	6
11–12	Viven Bessières grenade gun—in defensive	6
13	in offensive	6
14–15	Automatic rifle (fusil mitrailleur)	6
16–17	37 mm. gun ...	7
18–19	REQUIREMENTS TO OBTAIN BEST RESULTS OF NEW WEAPONS—	
18	(1) Combination ...	7
18	(2) Supply of ammunition ...	8
18	(3) Training ...	8
19	INCREASED POWER OF COMPANY RESULTING ...	8
	CONDUCT OF THE FIGHT—	
20–23	The section—	
22	(1) As assaulting unit	9
23	(2) As reinforcing unit ...	9
24–28	The company—	
24	Distribution	10
25–28	Plan of operations (17 sub-heads)	10

PARAS.		PAGE
29–37	The battalion—	
29	Distribution	12
30	Plan of operations—	
31	Clearing up captured trenches	12
32	Machine-gun company—	
	(1) At opening of attack	13
	(2) In course of attack	13
	(3) At occupation of conquered position...	13
33	37 mm. gun—	
	(1) At preparation of attack	14
	(2) In course of attack	14
	(3) At occupation of conquered position...	14
34	Plan of occupation of conquered ground (6 sub-heads)	14
35	Reconnaissance of further objectives and following up success	15
36	Refilling—	
	(1) Supplies	16
	(2) Ammunition	16
	(3) Stores	16
37	Inter-communication	16

SKETCHES ILLUSTRATING DISPOSITION.

No. 1.—1st Line Company in Attack Formation with two Assaulting Sections.
No. 2.—1st Line Company in Attack Formation with three Assaulting Sections.
No. 3.—Battalion in Attack Formation.
No. 4.—Plan of Action of Clearing-up Parties of the Battalion in Attack Formation shown in Sketch No. 3.

SUPPLEMENT TO INSTRUCTIONS ON THE OFFENSIVE OF SMALL UNITS.

Interior organisation of Companies and conduct of the Offensive by Small Units.

1. In order to secure a judicious training of the specialists of an infantry company and their proper use in battle, they must be grouped and organised. Some modification, therefore, is now required in the interior organisation of the Company.

As a result, moreover, of experience gained from the course of events, it is possible to issue precise rules for these specialists and for the combat of small units in general, complementary to the instructions issued 8.1.16.

The following notes give rules on these points and also specify the characteristics of the new infantry armament. They will be distributed right down to section commanders and will be brought to the knowledge of all concerned as widely as possible.

Organisation of a Company of Infantry.

2. The organisation and establishment remain as laid down in war establishments of 26.8.14.

3. For convenience the following designations will henceforth be recognised:—

Grenadiers (Bombers): Specialists in use of hand grenades and V.B.* grenade gun.

Fusiliers (Lewis Gunners): Specialists in the use of automatic rifle.†

Voltigeurs (Riflemen): The remainder of the company.

This last title is appropriate in view of the activity and devotion to varied duties required of.

These distinctions in no way alter the interior life of the company. All are equally available for work of every sort.

4. The company contains four similar sections. Each section is divided into two half-sections as follows:—

1st Half-section (under grenadier or fusilier sergeant):

No. 1 Squad (grenadiers)—1 corporal, sergeant and 7 grenadiers.

No. 2 Squad (fusiliers)—1 corporal and 6 fusiliers.‡

---

* Viven Bessières. (*Translator's Note.*—The V.B. grenade gun is used for firing rifle grenades.)

† Fusil mitrailleur.   ‡ Manning 2 automatic rifles.

2nd Half-section (under voltigeur sergeant):

   No. 3 Squad (voltigeurs)—1 corporal, 8 voltigeurs, 2 V.B. grenade gunners, 1 carrier.

   No. 4 Squad (voltigeurs)—1 corporal, 9 voltigeurs, 2 V.B. grenade gunners, 1 carrier.

5. Remaining supernumeraries, such as drummer, pioneer, &c., are distributed so as to equalise strength of squads. Not only the grenadiers, but every man, must be trained in grenade-throwing, and every " voltigeur " is in addition to learn some speciality.

6. Casualties in the 1st Half-section should be filled as a rule by the 2nd Half-section under arrangements of the company commander, approved by the commander of the battalion. The proportion of voltigeurs to grenadiers and fusiliers must not be allowed to fall too low.

Every effort should be made to retain the squad of voltigeurs complete.

This organisation will come into force at once.

Characteristics of the New Infantry Armament.

7. The following table shows the evolution of infantry armament since the beginning of the war:—

—	At beginning of War.	Present time.
Rifle and bayonet	Nearly total personnel.	—
Hand grenades	Nil	32 grenadiers per company.
Grenade guns	Nil	16 ,, ,, ,,
Automatic rifles	Nil	8 per company.
Machine guns	2 per company	8 per 3 companies.
37 mm. guns	Nil	1 per battalion.

Hand Grenades.

8. *In the Defensive*, can produce an excellent short-range barrage. In the hands of fearless, expert and well-provided grenadiers, they provide for the establishment of *centres of resistance* which are difficult to destroy, and which will afford protection to important features of the defensive line, such as salients, machine guns, outlets of communication trenches, &c. All except awkward men should be able to take their part in making a barrage at 30 yards' range; one man is required per 10 yards' frontage with the O.F., or one per 16 yards with the F. 1 grenade.

9. *In the Offensive*, the hand grenade will reach defenders under cover who have escaped the bombardment. It provides an excellent weapon for clearing out trenches and for working up communications.

10. The grenadier squad may be divided. This will often be necessary, especially when it is united with a fusilier squad to form a " wave."

Range, accuracy and discipline are the important points in grenade fighting. These result from training, and it is impossible to over-estimate their importance.

V.B. Grenade Guns (Rifle Grenades).

11. They may be employed as articles of trench equipment to harass the enemy, but are primarily for battle use.

12. *On the Defensive*, the 16 grenade rifles per company will project 150 grenades per minute and *automatically* set up an impassable barrage at 90 to 170 yards' range. Several grenade guns concentrated on a trench will stop hostile grenade throwing.

13. *In the Offensive*, the rifle grenade lengthens the zone covered by the hand grenade, and will reach an underground enemy at a considerable distance.

In the numerous local fights where artillery support is unobtainable the grenade gun supplies its place in the accurate bombardment of the enemy's centres of resistance. It cuts off hostile groups which are being attacked by hand grenades and prevents their retreat or reinforcement. Finally, it is most efficacious against hostile counter-attack.

In all situations, but more particularly in the offensive, it pays to employ concentration of fire with this weapon.

Automatic Rifles.

14. Characteristics :—
   (1) Extreme mobility.
   (2) Reliable effect at short distances. The fire is kept low automatically.
   (3) Fairly good effect at medium distances.
   (4) Considerable flexibility of control. Traversing fire can be carried out with facility. A change of objective can be made instantly.
   (5) Fire possible when in movement. Under certain circumstances the enemy may be compelled by this means to keep under cover at the time of the final rush to the assault.

The weapon has neither the rigidity nor rapidity of fire of the machine gun, and cannot altogether replace it. It resembles it, however, in moral effect. Moreover, it can accompany a small unit under circumstances where it would be impossible to set up a machine gun.

15. The automatic rifle, therefore, is pre-eminently the weapon to accompany infantry, for holding ground gained, and for stopping counter-attack. A great volume of fire is obtainable the very moment the objective is seized; the fire is flexible, and, furthermore, it gives time to bring up a machine gun deliberately and place it in a favourable position, particularly for flank defence.

In a captured position it can sweep communications along which the approach of the enemy's reserves may be expected. At this juncture it should be used as a preventive weapon to act on the enemy's moral and make his counter-attack come to nothing.

37 MM. GUN.

16. Characteristics :—
    (1) Enough mobility to enable it to accompany the infantry at all stages of the fight.
    (2) Extreme accuracy.
    (3) Ease of adjustment.
    (4) Effective range up to 1,600 yards.
    (5) Adapted to fire from a masked position.

The effects of the shell resemble those of a grenade, but it will penetrate two or three rows of sandbags, a timber blindage, or a steel plate before bursting.

This weapon is built to destroy any visible machine guns by direct fire.

It will also give good results against troops taken in enfilade.

17. Experience shows that this gun can seldom be used in the infantry "wave," as it is immediately spotted and destroyed.

Results to be obtained from the New Company Armament.

18. The best results will only be obtained from the newly constituted companies, provided three primary conditions are fulfilled :—
    1. The weapons must act in combination with one another.
    2. The supply of stores and ammunition must be ensured.
    3. The men must be expert in the use of these weapons.

(1) The *combination* of rifles, machine guns, automatic rifles, 37 mm. guns and rifle grenades forces the enemy to lie close in

their holes, whilst the grenadiers and voltigeurs hurl themselves forward and bring them to a hand-to-hand encounter.

The weapons of low trajectory (*i.e.*, rifle, machine gun, automatic rifle, 37 mm. gun) engage everything that shows above the ground, and the high trajectory weapons (hand and rifle grenades) engage everything that goes to earth.

The voltigeurs complete the results and follow up the successes obtained by the specialists.

(2) The perfect organisation of the *supply of stores and ammunition* is necessary in order to secure a sufficient supply for the various weapons at all times.

The heavy and cumbrous material, now required to keep the new weapons supplied, makes its provision all the more delicate an operation.

(3) *Training* is even more necessary with the new armament than with the old.

Arms of high efficiency are only effective when in the hands of disciplined and courageous experts, under officers with accurate knowledge of the weapons. All must get the idea out of their heads that specialists are a race apart, whose rôle in daily life and in battle is different from that of their comrades. These all live and fight in the same ranks and in close union with the voltigeurs. Their training only is specialised.

As this war goes on, the method of fighting is being continually modified; it is the duty of everyone to follow this evolution, and to take immediate advantage of every advance. With equal courage on either side, the best trained wins.

19. The present day company, with all its weapons and a proportion of machine guns in support, can produce a far greater volume of fire than could the same unit at the beginning of the war.

The difference is noticeable at medium distances, and is striking at distances under 200 yards. In the defensive the company can now hang on to its ground much more firmly whilst awaiting the protection of artillery barrage. This last property is particularly valuable to infantry during the period when, after the capture of an objective, the artillery has not yet obtained sufficiently exact knowledge of the situation to enable it to afford support.

In the offensive, infantry has regained the power and manœuvring ability which was so much reduced by the introduction of trench warfare.

Once the artillery has breached the enemy's defences the infantry can now dash forward into the latter and break up any local resistance of hostile counter-attacks with their own weapons.

Conduct of the Fight.

THE SECTION.

20. *The present method of fighting is characterised by a reduced density and increased depth of formation.*

Recent experience shows that an interval of four or five paces between men extended in line ensures the minimum of casualties without loss of cohesion.

This interval may be considered as the normal between riflemen; and, to avoid the loss of control resulting from overextension, the section should, from the first, be distributed in depth and not in breadth.

21. The normal fighting front of the section is from 80 to 100 paces. A section may take part in the fight :—

    (1) As an assaulting unit.
    (2) As a reinforcing unit.

22. *As an assaulting unit.*—(a) The first line, generally called "wave," usually consists of the 1st half-section (grenadiers and fusiliers).

The grenadiers deal with bodies of the enemy sheltering in trenches and shell holes.

The fusiliers direct their fire on any who show themselves, whether running back or advancing to counter-attack.

(b) The second line (or "wave") is formed by the 2nd half-section. The V.B. grenade gunners use their plunging fire to form a barrage either in front of the line they hold, or in rear of the line attacked; they may also bring fire to bear on the enemy under cover who are too far off to be dealt with by the hand grenade.

The voltigeurs follow up the first "wave" and use their rifles and bayonets to settle the fights commenced by their comrades.

The section commander moves with the second line between his voltigeur squads.

The distance between two "waves" varies from 10 to 15 paces.

Under certain circumstances there may be reason to place voltigeurs in the first "wave," particularly when the front of the section is greater than the normal. It is then advisable to employ them by squads to join up with the automatic-rifle squad.

23. *As a reinforcing unit.*—If strength admits, the section adopts a two-line formation like an assaulting section.

The section commander moves in front with his line of specialist squads, in a favourable position to guide his section according to the progress of events in front. He either deploys his squads or moves them in single file to keep them longer in hand.

When the supporting section is minus one of its specialist squads (as will be seen later) its commander may dispose it in a single "wave."

THE COMPANY.

24. *Distribution.*—The front allotted to the company varies from 220 to 330 yards.

The company is generally able to place two assaulting sections side by side in its battle front. It may also place three, and exceptionally four. Sections not forming part of the assaulting line become reinforcing sections.

The assaulting sections form the first two "waves" of the company ("assaulting waves"), which act as described in Section 22 above.

Immediately behind the "assaulting waves" come the parties for "clearing up" the trenches; these form the "*clearing up*" or third "wave" (v. further on). The remainder of the company (one or two sections less any detailed as "clearing up" party) form one or two "waves" according to strength, denominated reinforcing or manœuvring "waves."

The company commander moves at the head of the last mentioned. Reinforcing sections follow the "clearing up wave" at a distance of about 40 to 50 paces.

25. *Plan of operations.*—The success of an attack depends on the accuracy with which it is carried out. A commander should draw up his plans in such a manner as to ensure accuracy of execution.

The plan of operations is based on:—
 (1) The rôle assigned to the unit.
 (2) The obstacles to be overcome in order to ensure success.
 (3) The means at the disposal of the unit.

(1) The rôle of the unit and any supplementary means which may be placed at its disposal are detailed in the battalion commander's operation orders.

(2) The obstacles to be overcome are known nowadays in almost complete detail, thanks to excellent methods of observation and the information placed at the disposal of the troops by the Staff (*i.e.*, intelligence reports on the enemy's defences day by day, photographs, large scale plans, sketches, and information from various sources).

(3) All this information must be classified by the regimental commander, and useful extracts or reproductions freely distributed so as to reach all companies concerned. The company

commander issues the necessary copies to his subordinates, N.C.Os. included, and sees that each sketch shows the route and objective of the unit in coloured pencil.

26. The company commander issues the plan of operations for his company in the form of an operation order. This must be submitted for approval to the battalion commander without giving rise to paper work and correspondence.

27. The plan of operations details :—

(1) The rôle of the battalion, of the company concerned, and detached companies.
(2) The number of assaulting sections, the starting point of each, and its rôle and objective.
(3) The number and composition of " clearing up " parties and their respective rôles in accordance with the orders of the battalion commander.
(4) The distribution and respective rôles of reinforcing sections (from these the " clearing up " parties will be taken) and the routes they are to follow.
(5) Lines of attack of different units and their compass bearings.
(6) Distance between different echelons.
(7) Position of company commander.
(8) Time the assault is to start.
(9) Method by which the artillery fire is to be timed to conform with progress of the infantry.
(10) How the sections and company commander are to keep each other informed of their respective positions, especially the use of signalling devices (rockets, lights, &c.).
(11) Methods of communication with neighbouring units.
(12) The method to be adopted to mark out the front occupied either at some particular time or on some line agreed upon, or as required.
(13) The occupation of the conquered position, and following up the success obtained.
(14) Outfit to be taken.
(15) Supply of ammunition, including V.B. rifle grenades, and ammunition for automatic rifles and machine guns. Whether to be supplied under company or battalion arrangements; where these supplies will be drawn or delivered.
(16) Situation of store depôts for wire, sandbags, tools. &' required for the organisation of the new front.
(17) Evacuation of the wounded.

28. *Remark re Para.* 9.—The company commander must explain to the men how the artillery fire will lift as the assault progresses, and how in consequence the infantry must march, as

it were, into the shell fire, following up the barrage as closely as it is possible to do so. Officers with the attack carry no swords; they will be dressed and equipped like their men, with badges of rank as inconspicuous as possible.

THE BATTALION.

29. *Distribution.*—The battalion commander places one, two, or three companies in line according to the front allotted.

Companies in second line assume as thin as possible a march formation, moving to a great extent in line of squads in single file.

30. *Plan of operations.*—The battalion scheme is based on the same rules, and falls under the same heads as that of the company. In addition, the battalion commander issues orders for the following :—

(1) " Clearing up " the trenches.
(2) The employment of the M.G. Company.
(3) The employment of the 37 mm. gun.
(4) Occupation of the position won.
(5) Reconnaissance of a further objective, and following up the advantage gained.
(6) Replenishment of ammunition, &c.
(7) Intercommunication services.

31. *" Clearing up " of trenches.*—This is an extremely important operation, and must be carried out methodically and speedily. Courageous men are required and very energetic commanders.

The " clearing up " scheme is drawn up by the battalion commander according to instructions issued by the regimental commander. It is founded on aeroplane photographs, which show up the principal dug-outs of the enemy. With this assistance the battalion commander fixes the strength necessary to " clear up " each group of dug-outs, details the unit to furnish the detachments, and the duties of the latter when the " clearing up " is completed. As a rule, " clearing up " parties* are made up of grenadier squads reinforced by voltigeurs; they are always under the command of N.C.Os.

In some cases the strength of a party may be half a section or a section, and sometimes a complete company may be detailed to " clear up " some *point d'appui* of particular importance. " Clearing up " parties are never drawn from assaulting sections, which must be kept intact. They are drawn from reinforcing sections or from companies or battalions in second line.

---
* " Nettoyeurs."

When the objective of the first line companies consists of two lines of trenches some distance apart, it is indispensable to detail separate clearing parties for each group. But whatever their objective, the *whole* of these clearing detachments march in rear of the assaulting "waves."

Once their particular task is completed, the "clearing-up" parties may be employed on the preparation and occupation of the conquered trenches. In this case machine guns or automatic rifles are detailed to assist them. "Clearing-up" parties move in line or small columns, according to circumstances. Frequent drills in ",clearing up" trenches must be carried out.

32. *The machine gun company* is the powerful means at the battalion commander's disposal for completing by its fire effect the operations of his other units. He regulates its work—

(1) at the opening;
(2) during the progress of the attack;
(3) in the occupation of the objective assigned.

(1) *At the opening of the attack* the machine guns of battalions in the first line follow their battalions. They will be distributed at the discretion of the battalion commander, chiefly with a view to their installation on the captured front. The machine guns of the battalions in second line are placed, to begin with, on the front from which the attack starts. Placed at selected points affording good fields of fire, they may be employed to advantage in covering the flanks of the first line battalions by directing a stream of fire on any intervals which may occur between them, or more particularly on the outer flanks of the battalions on the wings of the whole force. When the shape of the ground permits, it is also desirable to bring these machine guns into action against the enemy's second or third lines, his communication trenches, or any machine guns which show themselves. But all necessary precautions must be taken to avoid hitting or obstructing our own troops.

(2) *When the attack is under way* the battalion commander sends all or part of his machine guns to positions which have been pointed out beforehand, and which offer the best facilities for securing the ground won either by his own battalion or those on either side.

(3) To keep a secure hold on ground when it is conquered the fullest possible use should be made of the various weapons, viz., machine guns, automatic rifles, and rifle grenades. Distribution on these lines will result in bringing the fusilier squads and grenade gunners (rifle bombers) into the first line occupied, and bring the grenadiers and voltigeurs into reserve to provide against counter-attacks. Furthermore, the battalion commander

must distribute his M.G. company and the fusiliers and grenade gun squads (rifle bombers) of the company or companies in reserve in such a manner as to increase the volume of fire available in the front line.

33. *The 37 mm. gun.*—This is, as a rule, a battalion weapon. In certain cases, however, the regimental commander may keep it in his own hands.

It is employed:—
  (1) To prepare and accompany the attack.
  (2) To break the resistance of enemy groups during the progress of assault.
  (3) To co-operate in the occupation of the position when conquered.

(1) *To prepare and accompany the attack.*—Before the attack starts the gun is mounted in an emplacement so as to act efficaciously either by destroying any M.G. emplacements disclosed at the last moment or by battering the second or third lines of the enemy. To avoid the destruction of the gun, it should only be brought into action at the last moment.

(2) *During the course of the attack* the 37 mm. gun goes forward when it can be of no further use in its initial position, or when it is required by the infantry to destroy some centre of resistance.

Its move must be provided for in the operation order.

On account of its vulnerability, it is never placed in the first "waves," but may accompany the battalion commander.

Its use is to destroy machine gun emplacements, or clear out fire or communication trenches when opportunities occur to enfilade them. Its employment too close to its target is to be avoided. Masked fire should be used as much as possible.

(3) *Occupation of the conquered position.*—The 37 mm. gun helps to secure a firm hold of a position won, in the same manner as a machine gun.

It is placed so as to bring fire (oblique for preference) to bear on the probable lines of approach of enemy counter-attacks. It is always advantageous to arrange to have more than one masked emplacement, so as to prevent the gun being easily spotted by the enemy's artillery.

34. *Plan of occupation of the conquered ground.*—It is based on the instructions of the regimental commander drawn up in accordance with the scheme laid down by higher authority.

It will provide for the following:—
  (1) Number of troops to be detailed to occupy the position.
  (2) Their distribution in breadth and more particularly in depth.

(3) The distribution of machine and 37 mm. guns.
(4) Works to execute; construction of fire and communication trenches; distribution of work to units.
(5) Information regarding sites of dumps of all sorts of stores, tools, wire, pickets, stakes, sandbags, &c.
(6) Approximate positions of different headquarters.

35. *Reconnaissance of further objectives and following up a success.*—The capture of the assigned objective is not the end of the battalion offensive.

It is, above all, necessary :—

To regain contact with the enemy.

To reconnoitre the enemy's new position.

To prepare and then carry out a forward movement with the idea of either securing a base of departure for a fresh advance, or of getting fullest possible value out of the success already obtained.

Contact is regained and the fresh position reconnoitred by patrols detached from the first line troops as soon as they reach the conquered position.

Their objectives are indicated in the orders for the attack.

These patrols are composed of grenadiers and fusiliers, strengthened by voltigeurs, who make their way rapidly towards their objectives. They occupy these objectives and form the skeleton of a fresh line to be occupied and organised as quickly as possible.

Full advantage should immediately be taken of any gaps in the enemy's defences.

Enterprising infantry will always find opportunities of completing an initial success by the seizure of *points d'appui* whose reduction would cost them dear the following day. It is particularly important to seize immediately any point which the enemy has abandoned.

The limiting of objectives does not imply the suppression of initiative.

The battalion commander must not lose sight of the fact that successes are not attained by the infantry alone, but by *combination with the artillery*. Ulterior progress, therefore, must be studied beforehand in communication with the artillery and worked out in fullest detail.

The necessity of sending back quick and frequent reports must be strongly impressed on all officers and N.C.Os.

36. *Replenishment of supplies, ammunition, and stores.*—The regimental and battalion commanders are responsible for the arrangements for these services.

Whatever may be the refilling arrangements, horse transport will invariably be brought as far forward as possible to avoid fatigue work to the troops. Donkeys and mules will be found most useful for the purpose.

(1) *Supplies.*—At starting, men will take all the food they can carry and three or four pints of water. Cooking and water carts, under charge of a very energetic officer or N.C.O., will be brought as close up to the troops as possible. Food of too liquid a nature for easy carriage is to be avoided. It is sometimes useful to employ a sort of squad ration basket containing the food for the whole of the following day. Preserved provision dumps may also be established at company headquarters. Solidified spirits of wine will be issued to the men for heating food.

(2) *Ammunition and signal lights.*—These are drawn from advanced dumps, each containing all descriptions of ammunition that can be asked for.

The development of the specialist services, leading as it does to a great consumption of weighty and bulky stores, makes the careful organisation of the refilling system of vital necessity.

A convenient arrangement is to make up ammunition into lots, each containing a proportion of :—

Rifle ammunition.
M.G. and automatic rifle ammunition, hand grenades.
V.B. gun grenades (rifle grenades).
Rounds for 37 mm. gun.
Rockets and signal lights.
Illuminating rockets.
Sandbags (for carrying stores).

When ammunition is demanded one complete lot is sent up in the absence of notification to contrary.

(3) *Stores.*—As in the case of supplies and ammunition, dumps should be placed close to the trenches from which the attack is to start, in the neighbourhood of company and battalion headquarters.

87. Intercommunication (references to other publications only).

Approved,
J. JOFFRE.

Sketch Plans.

The dispositions shown are merely explanatory. In practice they are to be modified according to circumstances.

1ST LINE COY IN ATTACK FORMAT[ION]

FRONTAGE

No 1. Section.

```
                  G G G     F F F  S₁  G G      F  F F F G G G -------┐
Assaulting Sections {                     c   G G       F F F G G G         20 pa[ces]
                                      S.C.                             c
                  v v v v v v v v   C gg gg gg gg C   v v v v v v v v ---------┤
                       c                                    c              15 pa[ces]
                                      S₂
                  Clearing up parties   G G G G      G G G G (Grenadier Squad of No 2 Sec[tion])
```

50 pa[ces]

No 2. Section.

```
                              S.C.                              Coy. Com[mander]
Reinforcing Sections { F F F     C gg gg gg gg C    F F F F -------(•
                                  S₁                                20 pa[ces]
                  v v v v v v v v                  v v v v v v v v -------
                       c                                c
                                  S₂
```

EXPLAN[ATION]

G   Grenadier. F_c Fusilier Corp^l.
G_c "   Corp^l.   V   Voltigeur.
F   Fusilier. V_c "   Corp^l.

⊙ Company C[ommander]

Sketch Nº 1.

...TION WITH 3 ASSAULTING SECTIONS.

220 YARDS.

Nº 3. Section.

```
┌----G G G G G G G G    F F F  S₁  F   F F F     v v v v v v v v
│                G                  C           (Voltigeur Squad of
ices                         S.C.                 second ½ section)
├------- v v v v v       C gg gg gg gg C          v v v v v
ices                         S₂
│        G G G G                       G G G G    Clearing up
├------                                            parties.
│       (Grenadier Squad of a Coy.
│              in 2ⁿᵈ line.)
ices
```

Nº 4. Section.

```
                            S.C.
nmander.
●------- F F F F F F F   C gg gg gg gg C   G G G G G G G G
              C                                      C
ices                        S₁
├------- v v v v v v v v                  v v v v v v v v
               C                              C
                            S₂
```

...IATIONS.

gg.	Rifle Grenade man.	S.C.	Section Commander.
C.	Carrier.	S₁	Sergt. of 1st ½ section.
		S₂	" " 2nd ½ section.

...ommander.

1ST LINE COY IN ATTACK FORMATI[ON]
(FRONTAGE 280

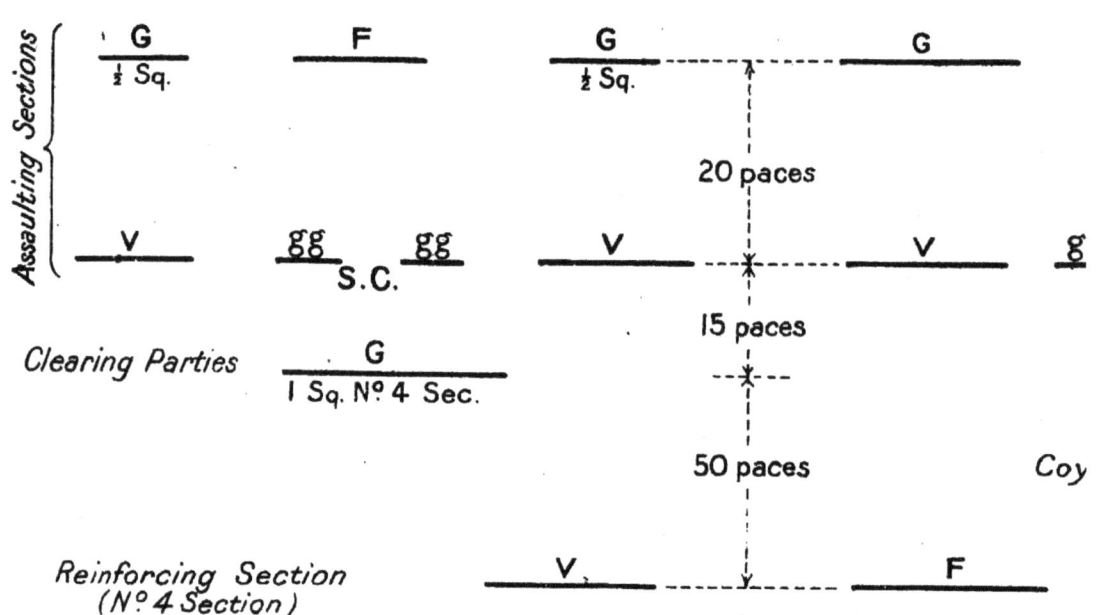

EXPLAN[ATION]

G. Grenadiers.

F. Fusiliers.

V. Voltigeurs.

P. Pioneers.

Sketch Nº 2.

ON WITH 3 ASSAULTING SECTIONS.

TO 330 YARDS)

| F   G   F   V |

g   gg   V   gg   gg   V
S.C. ――― ――V――   ――――   ――― ――― ―――
                                    ½ Sq.   S.C.   ½ Sq.

                    G
            ―――――――――――
            1 Sq. of a Coÿ of 2ⁿᵈ line

. Commander.
        ⊙
        R
―――   gg
S.C. ―――   ―――V―――
 P
―――

IATIONS.

gg.   Rifle Grenade men.

S.C. Section Commander.

R.   Runners.

BATTALION IN ATTACK FORMATION

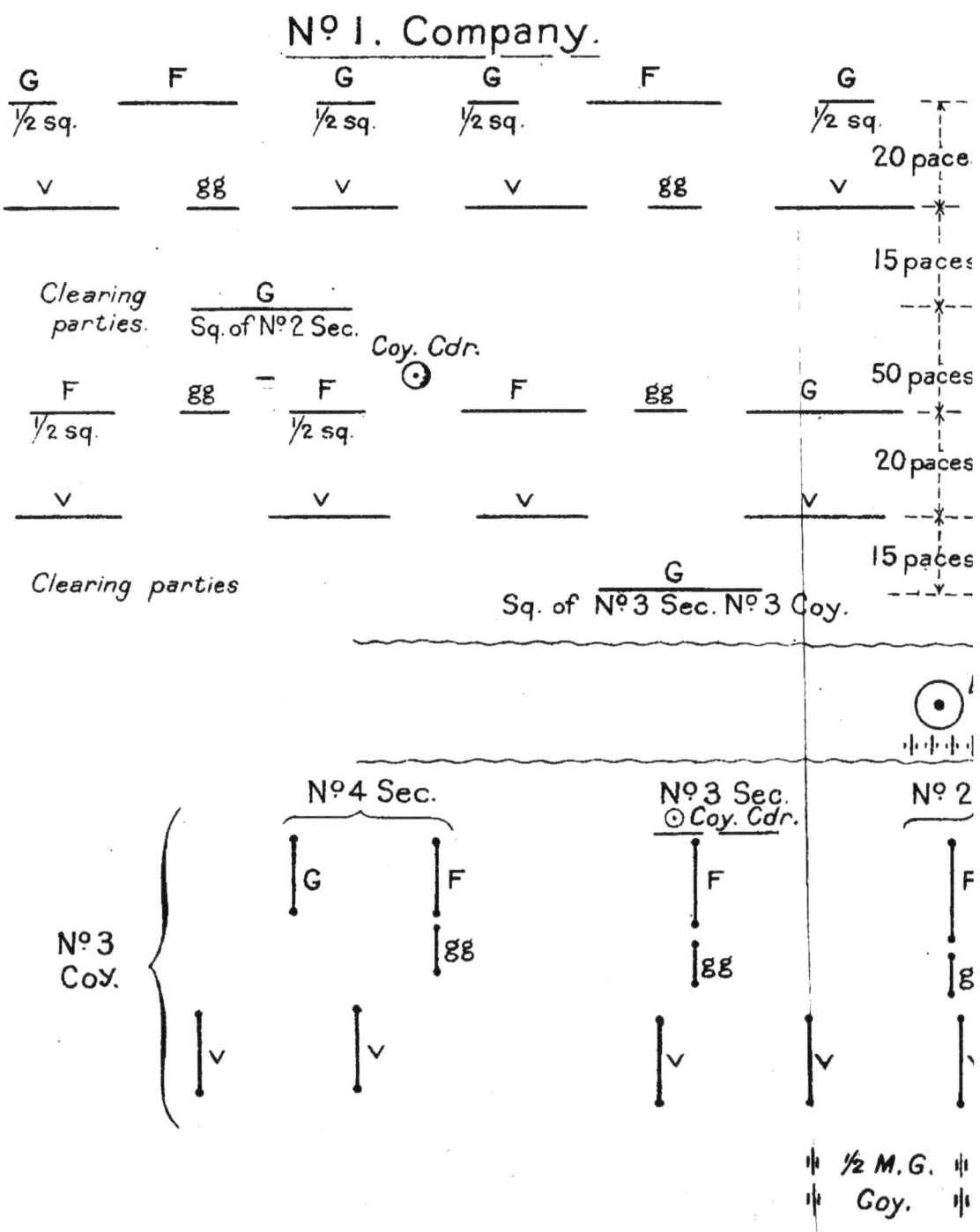

Sketch N°3.

N. (FRONTAGE 440 TO 550 YARDS.)

N°. 2. Company.

G	F	G	G	F	G	G	F	G
½ sq.		½ sq.	½ sq.		½ sq.	½ sq.		½ sq.

s

v   gg   v   v   gg   v   v   gg   v

G   G
Sq. of N°4 Sec.   Coy. Cdr.   Sq. of N°1 Sec. N°3 Coy.
                    ⊙

F   gg   F

v   v

G
Sq. of N°2 Sec. N° 3 Coy.

Bⁿ Comm^{dr}
½ M.G. Coy.

Distance of about 200 yards to N°3 Coy.

Sec.   N° 1 Sec.

F

gg

v   v   v   v

⊢⊣ 37 m.m. gun.

Malby & Sons. Lith.

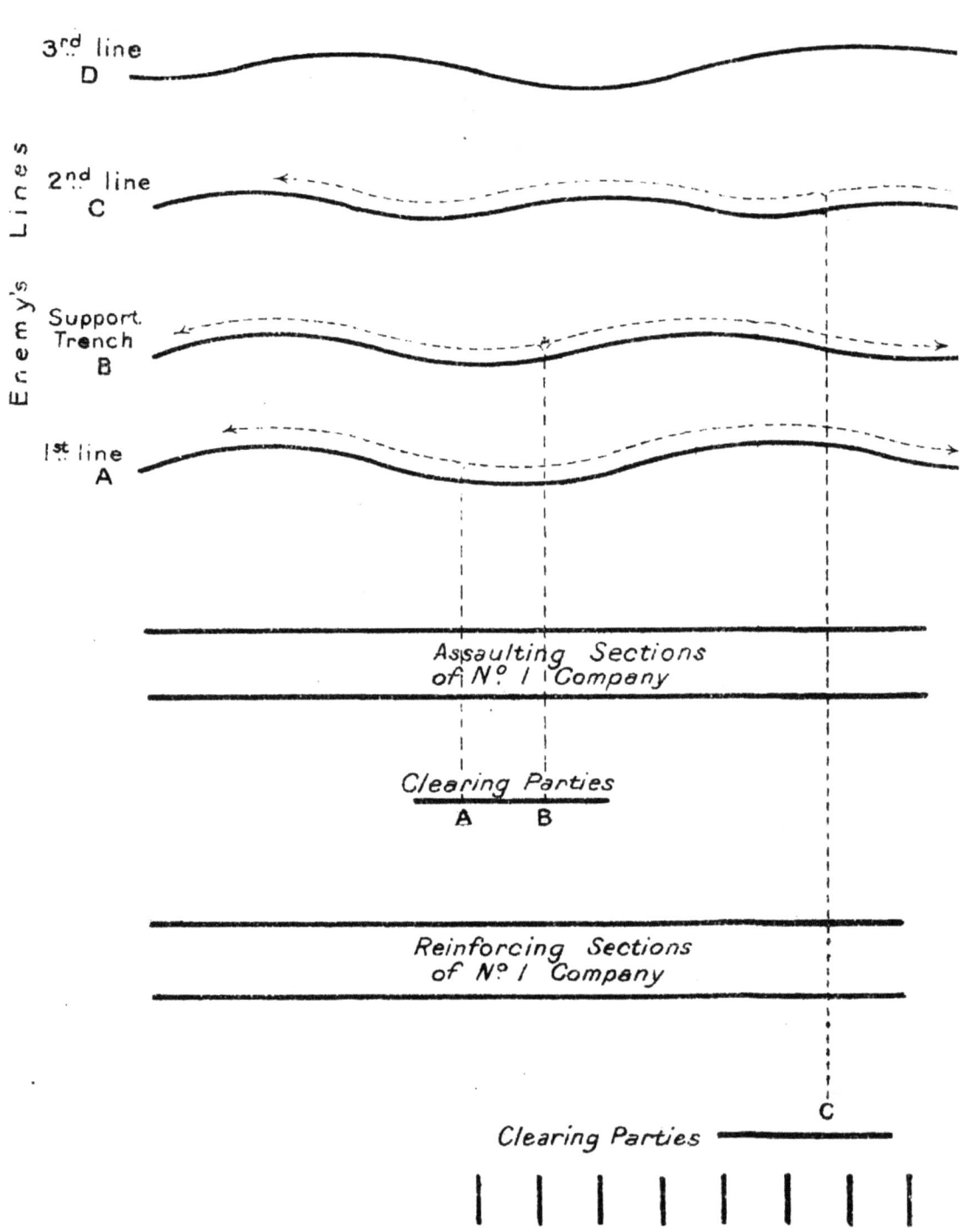

CLEARING UP PARTIES OF TENTION SHEWN IN SKETCH Nº 3.

Nº 4 Sketch

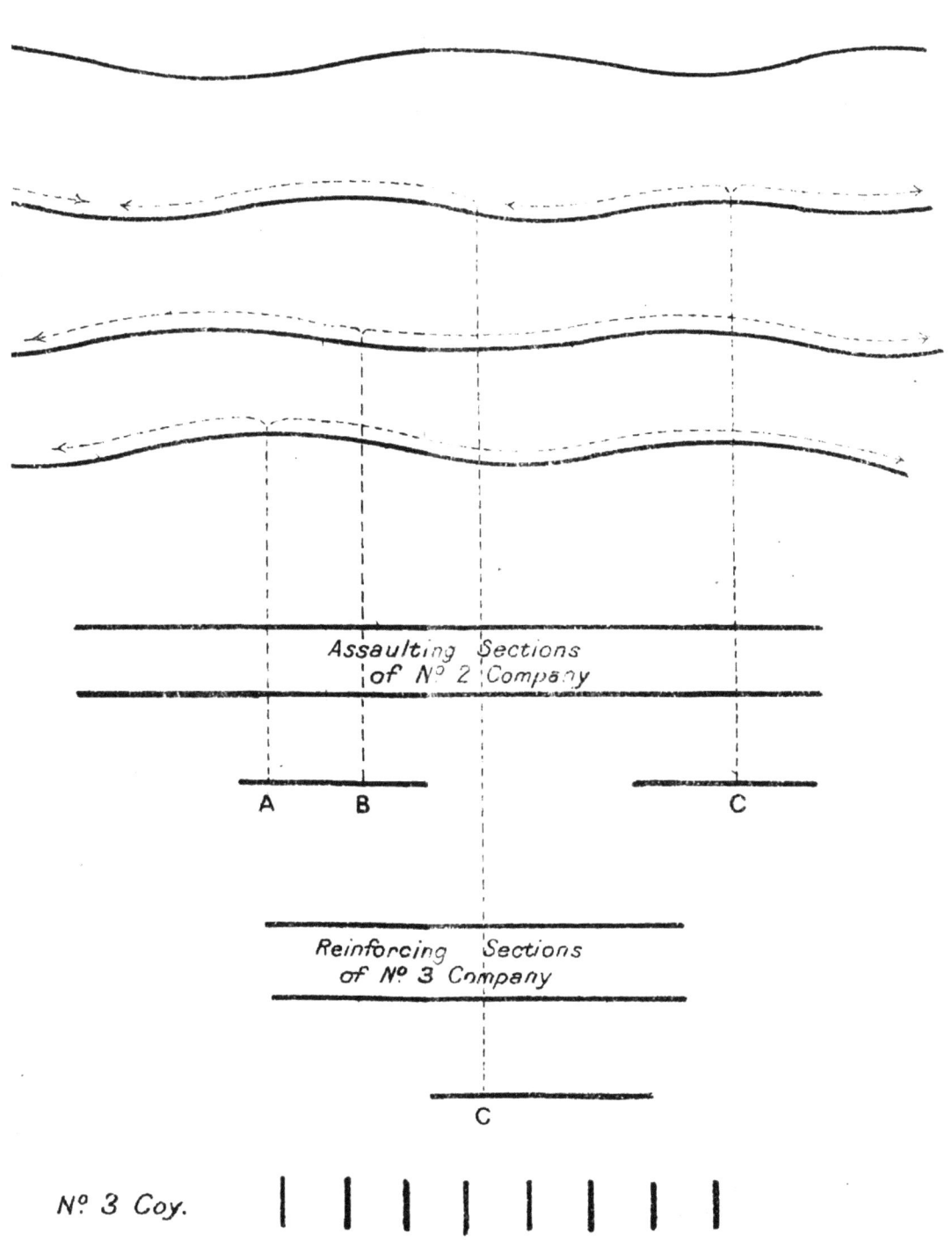

www.ingramcontent.com/pod-product-compliance
Lightning Source LLC
Chambersburg PA
CBHW060857090426
42736CB00026B/3500